Dr. Joe Vitale's

GREATEST LAW OF ATTRACTION QUOTES

Dr. Joe Vitale's

GREATEST LAW OF ATTRACTION QUOTES

DR. JOE VITALE

Hypnotic Marketing, Inc.
WIMBERLEY, TX

Cover design: Ted Angel
Editing & interior design: Tanya Brockett, www.HallagenInk.com

To Caroline

Contents

Introduction ix

Divinity 1

Inspiration 17

Counterintention Clearing 27

Gratitude and Giving 35

Wants, Needs, and Desires 41

Abundance vs. Scarcity 49

Dare to Take Control 57

Opportunities vs. Problems 65

Elevated Thinking 73

Wealth 81

Magic, Miracles, and Manifestation 89

Present Moment and Future Now 95

Self-Awareness... 101

Sources of Quoted Material 111

Introduction

Over the years, many of my quotes from training programs, movies, songs, and my many books have appeared on the social media feeds and print pages of others. Now, for the first time, I am collecting many of my own quotes that have inspired millions, and gathering them just for you.

These quotes have been repeated over many years of learning, growth, and transformation. If you have been following my work over time, you will find many that are familiar to you. Hopefully, they will put a smile on your face and remind you of miracles you have previously experienced. In reading these quotes, you may also find that, *"The opposite of a great truth is another truth."* As I collected these nuggets of wisdom for you, I became keenly aware that with the increase of time comes greater awareness; this truth is weaved throughout these pages. But isn't that part of the fun of our journey?

You will notice that this book is organized in loose categories so you can find what you need when you need it. I encourage you to read the book all the way through the first time. But then, I believe this book can be perfect for bibliotherapy: where you hold an intention in mind, open the book, and let the first quote you see become your oracle. Take its wisdom, and through inspiration, allow it to be just what you need.

As many others have done over the years with these and more quotes, feel free to cite them in social media with "Dr. Joe Vitale" as the source. If something stands out and resonates with you, it might also help someone else. Feel free to share.

Enjoy this collection and *Expect Miracles!*

Joe Vitale 2017

Dare something worthy. Do something with your life. Go for your dreams. Live your passion.

—DR. JOE VITALE

Divinity

The Divine knows better than you. The Divine always has something far better for you and so much more in mind for you than you can ever imagine.

If you were to pretend you could think like God, how would you think? What would you do? Think and act like God and you will realize that there truly are no limits.

The Universe loves you. It will support anything you believe. It's up to you to be in alignment with the Universe.

We live in a belief-driven Universe. Change your beliefs and you change your Universe.

Love is the foundation of everything. It's what we're seeking, what we're made of. It's directing everything in the Universe. Love is the driving force for life itself.

You are the creator of your life. You are in the driver's seat and you can co-create a happier life with the Divine by your side.

We are all connected. We're nothing but energy and we're all one.

Trust that the Divine is orchestrating all the events in your life for your highest good. We just don't know the end plan.

Give up needing to know how you will manifest anything; surrender control and free the Universe to bring you whatever you want.

"Thank you, Universe, for all the blessings I have in my life and all the blessings I am receiving." Say this to yourself every day. Say it often.

You don't need to know how the Universe will rearrange itself to manifest your desire. You really don't need to know how it's going to come about.

The Universe is like a movie camera. Think something, feel something, and the Universe will pick it up and project it.

Trust that when something happens, it's good; and trust that when something you want doesn't happen, it's good too.

Inspired action works because it comes from a bigger picture—the Universe. Your ego can only see limited terrain, while the Universe can see it all.

When you do what you love, you get on a track that seems like it was set up for you a long time ago by the Divine. The Divine pulls all the strings and the rest of the Universe makes everything happen for you.

You truly attract success when you get out of your ego and its petty desires, and instead allow the Divine to direct your way.

The Universe sees the bigger picture. Your ego only sees a tiny sliver of what is possible, and that's why it can't control your future.

Orders from the Divine trump all other commitments.

When you surrender to a higher power, you end up with more power than you ever had before.

When you change your life and live a "life of demonstration," you can be an inspiration for somebody else.

When you live from your heart, the Divine comes in and orchestrates everything, putting you on a path that was destined for you. Life becomes magic and miracles.

The more you listen to your inner nudges, the easier your life becomes.

—DR. JOE VITALE

Inspiration

Inspiration is knocking on your door right now. It's trying to send you a message. Be open to receive it. The Universe is always sending signals to you to take inspired action.

An idea is a message and an inspiration to you from the Divine. When an idea comes to you, honor it by writing it down or recording it. You will attract more ideas by "honoring the muse."

Intentions rule the Earth. It causes the Universe to rearrange everything and everyone around you to help you fulfill your intentions.

The more you listen to your inner nudges, the easier your life becomes.

You can virtually turn your life around by focusing on what you want with feeling and acting in an inspired way to bring it to you.

When an inspired idea comes to you, honor it by acting on it. A new idea that comes into your awareness is actually a gift and a blessing from the Universe.

Intention rules! You can float with circumstances life brings you, or you can create your own direction and circumstances. It all begins with a decision. What do you want? Decide. Choose. Declare.

Are you a writer? Do not edit as you write your first draft. It will cripple your creativity. Let go of the editorial process, write on impulse, and allow creativity to flow in.

Your intention is the most powerful when you are the most clear about it. You are the power of intention.

When you get the nudge to do something, DO IT. Action is how you magnetize yourself to attract what you want. It's your part in the manifestation process.

As you grow, your dreams and desires will change. Don't be afraid to jump on new opportunities that inspire you.

Intention is not as important as inspiration. Intention is a toy of the mind; inspiration is a directive from the Divine. The goal is to listen, receive inspiration, and ACT, not to beg and wait.

Do what you love. When you follow your heart, you seem to be moving into alignment with the Universe, and the Universe will reward you.

In order to inspire others, you must allow yourself to be inspired.

Drop the fear. Drop the ego. Come from inspiration. Follow inspiration. And trust what unfolds.

It's not your motivation that will produce results —it's your inspired action.

Follow your hunches, watch the signals, and listen to your intuition. If you get a desire to make a plan of action, do it!

Your inspiration is as available as your next breath. You just have to look within yourself and say, "Okay, if I was carefree and everything was paid off..." or "If I was a child again, what would I be doing?"

If you dared something worthy, if you really went for your biggest and boldest dreams, what would you want? That's where your passion would start to kindle.

Ego intentions are "comparison-winner" driven and come from your head, whereas Divine intentions begin with an intuitive nudge felt in the heart and are "passion-enthusiasm" driven. You want to focus on your Divine intentions.

Look within yourself to find your inspiration. When you were a child, what did you say you wanted to do when you grew up? What was your hobby? What did you do for fun?

Make yourself really excited and maybe a little bit nervous by going for something that is bigger than you thought before.

Passion is the ticket to success. Follow your passion and you're on the road that's right for you.

Ride the enthusiasm that a new idea brings in and act on it before the initial excitement disappears.

Something magical happens when you state your intention. You realign the forces within yourself, your whole body and mind, to go in one particular direction towards a new target.

Do what you want to do in a way that honors you, honors your passion, honors the moment, and honors your heart.

State your intentions with emotion and feeling. Your strong intentions have the power to override your unconscious tendency to block your own good, and end the self-sabotage.

Stop figuring out how you will get what you want. Just follow your inner promptings and act on opportunities that come your way, and you'll get there.

The doorway to bliss is following your passion. Your passion is your direct connection to the Universe.

The inspiration to do anything needs to come from your heart or your gut, not your mind. When you follow inspiration, you get to say, "I'm on a mission from God."

Don't pursue money; pursue your passion, whatever is pumping through your veins that says, "This is exciting."

The real key to success is your passion. When you follow that deeper rush of energy within you, it's pointing you to your Divine Path.

Act on your inner nudges. Your intuitions and impulses will take you in a direction of creating or attracting the thing that you want to manifest.

The Universe likes speed. Don't delay. Don't second-guess. Don't doubt. When the opportunity is there, when the impulse is there, when the intuitive nudge from within is there, ACT. That's your job. And that's all you have to do.

When you do what you love, it doesn't feel like work. You won't feel as if you are going up the rocky road of a mountain to get to your success; you are on an escalator and everything seems so easy.

Are you acting on the nudges you get, even when you have no idea where they will lead? If so, you will find life exhilarating.

When you follow your inspiration, your life becomes effortless. It's almost like your guardian angels have come floating down and are paving the way for you.

You don't manufacture your outcomes—you participate in them. And you participate best when you allow you inner spirit to do most of the work.

As you go through life there are signs to go forward, pause, or even stop and retreat. The key is to pay attention to the clues and act on them. When you do, life seems to flow at a smooth rate.

You want to honor the desires welling up from deep within you, the wishes that are from your core. When you come from that place of nothing-is-impossible, you can have anything you imagine.

Your intention should come from your inspiration and not your ego. Inspiration comes from who we really are and intention comes from who we think we are.

"I Love You," "I'm Sorry," "Please Forgive Me," and "Thank You" are the four most powerful phrases that clear all your limiting beliefs and erase all the negativity inside of you.

—DR. JOE VITALE

Counterintention Clearing

Always remember this formula: the beliefs that you have, lead to the actions that you are taking, which lead to the results that you are getting. Understand your beliefs and clear all the limiting and negative ones.

The "Missing Secret" in *The Secret* is getting clear of the blocks, beliefs, and limitations within you at the unconscious level. Once you get clear, then you truly can have, be, and do whatever you want.

Don't fight a negative emotion. If you resist it, you give it the power to reoccur. Acknowledge it and let it go. It will dissipate and evaporate.

Your life can be fantastic if you clear the limiting beliefs within you. You have to take care of the inner world before the outer is resolved.

Forgiveness is incredibly powerful and begins with you. It is the understanding that nothing bad has happened in the first place, and the assumption that it all happened for your highest good.

Gratitude is an amazing clearing method because it melts down everything within you that resists you being okay with the present moment. As you are more grateful for what you have, you will get more of what you desire.

The point of life is to awaken and become fully conscious. We want to clean the unconscious of all limiting or negative programming so we can be in the divine flow that brings us magic and miracles.

Four phrases that erase the negative programming within you and clear your beliefs at the unconscious level, where you attract things that you don't want, are: "I Am Sorry," "Please Forgive Me," "Thank You," and "I Love You."

Forgiveness is so amazingly liberating; it's cleaning your mind and body so you can have, do, or be anything you want.

Whatever happens in your life, no matter how it got there, is up for healing simply because it is now on your radar.

When you forgive anybody whom you hold a grudge against, and when you forgive yourself, you release energy stuck inside you to open up a flow of love that brings you back to this point of power, this moment, now.

Your inner limiting beliefs are just thoughts you've infused with your own energy. They are not facts. As you release them, you get rid of your mental blocks and allow success to come into your life.

Get clear. Being clear means you are consciously and unconsciously in alignment with your desire. You don't have any counterintentions stopping you from attracting what you want.

Clearing our inner, limiting beliefs is a lot like peeling the layers of an onion. We have to keep removing the programming to reach the clarity of our source and become one with the Universe.

Don't fight with your reality. Accept your reality. Relax into your current situation and neutralize all the negative energy that pulled it into your being in the first place.

Forgive yourself now. Most of us treat ourselves horribly. If our best friends were to talk to us the way that we talk to ourselves in our own minds, we would fire them and disown them.

To change a bad habit, burn your bridges with it. Make it impossible to go back to the old habit or way of being.

Let go of the idea that you must complete everything you start because sometimes what you learn part-way through that one idea leads to an even better one.

"I Love You" "I'm Sorry" "Please Forgive Me" "Thank You" are the four most powerful phrases that clear all your limiting beliefs and erase all the negativity inside of you.

Feelings aren't sneaking up on you unannounced; they are available for your control. Change your thoughts and you'll change your feelings.

Your conscious mind is a tiny little drop in the ocean. Your unconscious mind is the ocean that has all of the beliefs, cultural programming, and brainwashing which needs cleaning up.

When you "get clear" of the hidden beliefs that are your inner obstacles or counterintentions that stop you from attracting whatever you want, you get what others may call miracles.

To paraphrase the Buddha—Life is suffering, but once you realize this, you no longer have to suffer. You are free.

We are human "beings," not human "doings." When you reach a clear inner state of being about your service to the world, the world will come to you.

"I Love You," are the three most powerful words that you can say to anybody, including yourself. Use them often. Use them now.

Once you feel grateful, you are in an energy that can create miracles.

—DR. JOE VITALE

Gratitude and Giving

God has given you life because you deserve it.

Gratitude is a wonderful tool to appreciate the present moment. The more you feel grateful, the more you attract new moments to be even more grateful.

Give recklessly with a deliriously open heart without concern for receiving. As you give, the world's heart opens, and all are blessed—including you.

When you focus on something that you are genuinely grateful for in this moment, you transform your whole energy, you feel and think differently, and your whole state of being is changed.

If you give freely without expecting anything in return, you'll receive back in kind many times over.

If you want to turn your life around right now, start making a list of all the things to be grateful for. This will shift your energy and take your focus off your problems.

Every week, reflect on who or what inspired you or fed you spiritually that week and give 10% of your income to that person or organization.

As soon as you start to feel differently about what you already have, you will start to attract more of the good things, more of the things you can be grateful for.

The more people you help, the more money you attract. If you want more, serve more.

One of the lost secrets to success is giving. When you give, you begin a pattern to begin getting.

Think of money as a beloved tool whose sole purpose is to express appreciation. The more you feel appreciation, the more you will attract in the next moments more things to appreciate.

What you put out in the world comes back to you several times over.

You are wealthy right now. You are doing far better than you imagine. What you are striving for is "more." One of the ways to start attracting "more" in your life is to feel grateful NOW.

When you support a cause that you believe in, you start to get outside of your mental limitations and expand your ability to receive to yourself.

When you feel appreciation, you begin to attract more to appreciate. To attract money, appreciate money and what it brings you.

If you have a dollar, give a dime. If you have a dime, give a penny. The act of giving starts the process of receiving.

When you feel that money is good, and you are good, and you are continually grateful for the money that comes into your life (and grateful for the money that goes out of your life, too!), this allows you to do the things that make money come to you.

You activate the greatest money-making secret in history when you give freely, joyously, to wherever you get spiritual nourishment and nurturing.

Once you feel grateful, you are in an energy that can create miracles.

When you give anything, you tap into a higher spiritual law. You have little to do but give, wait, and receive.

A goal should scare you a little, and excite you a lot.

—DR. JOE VITALE

Wants, Needs, and Desires

Anything you fear or love will tend to be attracted into your life. Choose what you want to attract wisely.

You must love the thing that you wish to attain. Nothing but intense love will enable you to surmount the many obstacles placed in your path and to bear the burdens of the task.

When you are clear about what you want, Heaven and Earth seem to move in the most unpredictable ways to make the most seemingly impossible things happen.

"I intend" is more empowering than "I want." Stating your intention is much stronger than just wanting something.

It's not the thing you want. It's the feeling that it gives you.

There is nothing wrong with demanding what you want from the Universe. The clearer you state your intentions, the better your results will be.

You can attract what you want faster if you don't need it. When you state your intention and let it go, you give your unconscious mind and the Universe a chance to begin working on bringing it to you.

You have to want what you want and not want what you want at the same time. This is the truth of the Universe.

When you want to attract something into your life, detachment is the key. You can have anything you want as long as you don't need it.

Add the power of emotion to your mental imagination while attracting what you want. Feeling accelerates the process of attraction.

When you put too much need on a goal or intention, you push it away. Your desperation sends out a signal in the Universe that "I don't believe this is real." The key to success is wanting more without needing more.

Freedom and power come from knowing what you want without being a prisoner to what you want.

The quest for materialistic stuff is a grand illusion. There's nothing wrong with wanting the stuff, as long as you know that it's only a part of the game of life and is not going to bring you lasting happiness.

We have to let go of all blame, attacking, and judging to free our inner selves to attract what we want. Until we do, we are gerbils in a cage chasing our own tails and wondering why we aren't getting the results we seek.

The Universe will give you what you want if you ask for it with detachment and love, and you're in alignment to receive it.

"Alignment" means your conscious and unconscious minds want the same thing. *Anything* will work when you are in alignment with your goals.

A thought is powerful only if it is backed by feeling. Feeling is what helps Law of Attraction to get everything you want into your experience faster than you might have ever imagined.

Emotion has the power to create what you want. The energy in the emotion will work to pull you toward the thing you want, while also pulling the thing you want toward you.

Attracting what you want in your life can be really fun! It's like having the Universe as your catalogue and placing your order. It's really that easy.

A goal should scare you a little, and excite you a lot.

If you are detached from the outcome while practicing Law of Attraction, you increase the odds of receiving what you want, because you don't have a counterenergy going out sending an "energy of need" in the Universe.

You get more of what you focus on. If you want wealth, focus on wealth. If you want health, focus on health. If you want happiness, focus on happiness.

A scarcity mind sees the problem; the abundant mind sees the product or service or solution. Which mindset do you want to embrace?

—DR. JOE VITALE

Abundance vs. Scarcity

Your perception creates your reality. You can look at life and see scarcity or abundance. It depends on your mindset.

We create our lives out of our perceptions. If we focus on lack, we get more lack. If we focus on riches, we get more riches. Our perception is a magnet.

In every moment you have a choice: you can see the limitation before you, or you can see the abundance before you.

Shifting your focus to where you want to be, rather than focusing on what you don't have, shifts you out of the scarcity mindset and into receiving mode.

The more you can drop all the walls of fear and all the walls of lack and limitation, the more you can be abundant right now. Abundance is in this moment.

The scarcity view of the world worships money. The abundance view worships passion. When you focus on doing what you are passionate about, money will follow.

There is no scarcity in the Universe. Scarcity exists in our scientific understanding of the Universe, in our own psychological makeup, and in our belief system.

There really isn't any shortage in the world. The Universe is bigger than our egos and can supply more than we can demand.

There is enough for everybody. When everybody starts to live from their hearts, and go for what they want, they don't all want the same person, thing, or experience.

The thing is, we have so much baggage around money that we can't follow our dreams or let others follow theirs. Money is neutral. It's simply a way to transact business so you can pursue your dreams while others pursue theirs.

You never have to worry about money. Worrying about money doesn't ever help. Worry will not propel you to take action, it doesn't solve your problems, and it definitely doesn't help you to attract or manifest. Worrying is, simply, the worst thing you can do when you're broke.

The world is not about competition and scarcity. It's about cooperation and abundance.

There is true magic and miracles in the world. There is true abundance in the world. And you can start to see it when you choose to see it. So what are you seeing right now?

You can do the impossible. What you believe to be the restraints of time and space right now may simply be the limits of your current understanding.

I think each one of us has a limit we've placed on our freedom to think BIG. In reality, even the sky is not the limit.

The ultimate freedom is to never worry about where money is coming from, to know that it will just flow to you with your thoughts and beliefs about your sense of deservingness.

Come from abundance, not scarcity. Give without expecting anything in return. Go from a poverty mindset to a prosperity mindset.

You don't have to be "efforting" through life when you can be flowing through life.

Can you imagine having a relationship with a person the way that you have a relationship with money? You ignore it most of the time, you don't like to talk about it, and anytime you directly address money, it's only to complain or to worry about it. That is not a healthy relationship, and it will make money stay away from you.

The Universe comes from a place of love and support. The Universe is saying "yes" to you right now. If you align your unconscious mind with it, you will attract abundance in your life.

When you realize that everything is an "inside job," you will find that switch within you that transforms your life to one full of abundance and miracles.

When you have a positive prosperity mindset, then almost anything you decide to pursue will succeed. The whole idea of attracting money is to enjoy your life.

True prosperity is an incredible gift. It's a gift *you* deserve. And no matter what anyone says, it's a gift that *is* available to you—right now.

You can have, do, and be anything you want.

Expect miracles and you will attract miracles. Nothing is impossible or incurable or too good to be true.

Do the thing you wish, and walk through the fear.
On the other side is freedom.

—DR. JOE VITALE

Dare to Take Control

Dare something worthy. Do something with your life. Go for your dreams. Live your passion.

Almost all first steps are awkward. The same way you learned to walk is how you learn to do anything. Take some stabs at it. Walk a little, wobble, fall down, and get up again.

The secret to handling failure is to accept that "Nothing bad ever happens to you." Failure is not death.

We are on autopilot, running by the beliefs that we have inherited from our family, culture, and media. It's time to awaken and take conscious control over our lives.

Always remember that *you are in control*, because you may tend to forget that a lot throughout your life.

You have to take 100% responsibility for everything in your life. That's when you become the God of your life. That's where the real power is.

To achieve goals you've never achieved before, you may need to rise in levels, step out of your comfort zone, and participate with new people on a new playing field.

The three magic questions to get clear about anything: What would I do if I weren't afraid? What would I do if money were no object? What would be better?

What would you do if you could not fail? What would you do if you were fearless and could do anything? Get into that feeling, feel the end result, relish this empowered state of mind, and take action.

When you are clear about what you want, and willing to do whatever it takes to achieve it, the action you take will be effort free.

Dare something worthy and you unlock the powers of yourself and All That Is. Dare something worthy today.

If you don't act now, why not? Whatever your answer, that's an excuse.

Leave your excuses behind, and you will begin to attract wealth.

Most of the wealth that you want will probably come from the area of your life that you are afraid of.

Breathe through your fears; a lot of them dissolve just in taking inventory of them.

Transcend your fear and dare something worthy in your life by focusing on what you want. Fear will only stop you if you let it.

When you consider doing something that's daring and worthy in your life, you will ignite that passion; you'll be coming from a place of inner fire. You'll pretty much dissolve anything in the way for you to go and achieve it.

Face up to what you need to do and face it without fear. Let go of fear and give yourself permission to enjoy your life while improving it.

Think Big! Dare Something Worthy! You can attract wealth when you are fearless. Your wealth may be hiding right behind the very thing you are reluctant to do.

It is important to face your fears, because behind them are treasures.

Never give up! You have to try everything before you quit. No one knows what will work, or not. Testing is the great God.

Do the thing you wish, and walk through the fear. On the other side is freedom.

You must never quit! When you work towards any big goal, it's normal for your motivation to ebb and flow. But it's your persistent action that will produce results!

The challenges in your life are there to shake you up to do something different, transcend your fears, and do something worthy! 'Aude Aliquid Dignum'—Dare Something Worthy.

Problems are opportunities in disguise. Undress them to see the solution. Inside every challenge is the resolution to that challenge.

—DR. JOE VITALE

Opportunities vs. Problems

Some of the greatest challenges that you are facing right now can become future opportunities. Hold this thought in your mind and try to find good in every bad situation.

Being backed into hardship is good for the soul. It causes you to look for new solutions and change poor habits, behaviors, and thinking. It causes you to look within.

Circumstances don't make you. You make you. The bad times might become the greatest period of prosperity for you.

The economic downturn should be like a spiritual kick in the butt to bring about a change in our lives! We have to quit looking on the outside and start looking on the inside.

It isn't the successes, for the most part, that teach you things; it is the failures. A failure really isn't a failure. A failure is an educational success.

Most of your life's lessons will come from your failures and not your successes.

What looks horrible in the moment usually looks good a few years from now. Look for the good in the bad. It's there.

Problems are opportunities in disguise. Undress them to see the solution. Inside every challenge is the resolution to that challenge.

Instead of looking at the problem, look for the solution and TIISG: "Turn it into something good."

When your world seems really chaotic, it's actually good. It means something new is being restructured. It is forcing you to try something new and do something different.

The trick is in turning every one of your complaints around to something you *do* want. So "I don't want to struggle in my business" will become "I want business to come to me easily and effortlessly."

Know what you don't want. Because that's the springboard of knowing what you *do* want.

Don't talk yourself out of an idea just because it's been done before. Put your own spin on it. Bring in your own personal experiences. You will have your own stories to tell, which will make it unique.

Doing something that you've never done before is like putting on a new pair of shoes. Very often you get blisters; however, your skin will heal, it will toughen you, and you'll be walking around with new shoes, feeling optimistic, abundant, and looking forward to the future.

Challenges are good. They are causing you to look deeply within yourself and come up with creative solutions to awaken from the very thing that caused the problems, to transcend everything, and create a better life.

Excuses are beliefs. If you buy into them, you're stuck. If you believe that there's always a way around whatever the excuse is, then you'll move forward because "There is *always* a way."

The economy has nothing to do with your well-being and prosperity. It's how you perceive your reality and the opportunities around you.

Attracting money has nothing to do with having the right education and knowing the right people. It has everything to do with your mind and your beliefs about money.

Some of the greatest millionaires were built and created during a great depression.

Ask yourself what you would do even if you were never paid. That's a clue to what you should be doing, and of course finding a way to be paid for it.

Listen. Act. Prosper. There are opportunities around you. Which will you see first and act on now?

Economic recessions and depressions have always produced enormous opportunities for people willing to ignore the negativity.

Your perception about money determines whether it is a gift or problem. The choice is in your mind. Money will match your mindset.

While you may always desire to achieve the goals you stated, always remind yourself that whatever the outcome, you succeeded in some way.

Everything in your life is happening for your highest good. It's all good. It's all good.

—DR. JOE VITALE

Elevated Thinking

Loving yourself is the greatest path to improving yourself. And as you improve yourself, you improve your world.

Whatever you say after "I am" defines who you become.

Elevate your goals so that they are spiritually based where there are no limits, and not ego based where there are limits due to Earth's level of awareness of what's possible.

If you can be happy in this moment, you'll have achieved whatever you want. You don't need anything else in order to be happy right now. You can choose to be happy.

You can move mountains with the right thought and action. Keep a balance of ego and spirit in your life, always striving to let your ego obey spirit.

Most of us expect problems. What if we expect miracles? You will experience a dynamic shift in your consciousness that teaches you to look only for the good.

There is no competition. There is no enemy. There is only the desire to improve yourself. As you improve, the world improves.

You are the masterpiece of your own life; you are the Michelangelo of your experience. The David that you are sculpting is you, and you do it with your thoughts.

If you expect outside forces to help you, you'll see opportunities. If you expect outside forces to harm you, you'll see problems.

Try to find positive in the negative, and trust that there is positive there, even if you can't see it in the moment.

You can't stop your thoughts. But you don't have to listen to them, either.

Monitor your thoughts, notice the negative ones, and consciously replace them with positive ones.

The ego gets a big rush out of struggle. But the truth is, you don't have to struggle at all when there is always an easier way to achieve whatever you want.

When the world seems bleak, when you feel out of sorts, when your body feels tired and your mind seems wild, sometimes all you need is a good nap.

You have simply absorbed the beliefs that you were given when you were a child. It's time to awaken. You have a choice; you can choose to let go of the beliefs you don't want, and replace them with ones that better serve you.

Negative news is like a disease, and you can choose to allow yourself to be infected or not.

It's really important that you feel good, because this feeling good is what goes out as a signal into the Universe and starts to attract more of itself to you.

When your mind asks, "What if?" and plays a negative movie in your mind, change it by asking, "What if?" and play a positive scenario.

Assume every moment is your turn-around one, and act from that perspective. Life would then take on a glow.

You can motivate yourself for change with a decision and with the leverage to succeed. Create a win-win for yourself, knowing that you cannot fail.

Life doesn't have to get you down. There's a secret to feeling better: breathe slowly, deeply, completely, and sigh.

If you created this moment based on previous thoughts and actions, what will your next moments be, based on your current thoughts and actions? If you want to change the results, you need to change your thoughts and actions.

Don't doubt your current reality or argue with the present moment. We have to trust that we are in the right place and going in the right direction without judgment.

We are all born into victimhood. You are programmed to think about life in a particular way. You are taught how to survive, and not taught to thrive or prosper. You need to reprogram your life with positivity to feel empowered and get rid of the victim mentality.

Start thinking of money like a Monopoly game. It's just a game that does not determine your happiness or worthiness. It's neutral and independent of your self-esteem and self-worth.

Money will always match your mindset.

Agreeing to life is the great secret to life; not controlling life.

To achieve a positive mindset, turn off the mainstream news and quit listening to the negative people in your life.

There is no such thing as perfection. It is a very subjective interpretation. Do not get caught up in achieving perfection.

If you like this moment, dwell on it, as it will soon be gone. If you don't like this moment, relax, as it will soon be gone.

Everything in your life is happening for your highest good. It's all good. It's all good.

Your wealth is hiding under the very thing you are afraid to do. It's time to face your fears and take action. Expect Miracles.

—DR. JOE VITALE

Wealth

Money is an invisible energy system that we agree on as a means of exchange. There is no lack, limitation, or scarcity. When you need money, you just need to dip into the well of prosperity and pull it or attract it to you.

People often think that they will have a wealth mindset once they have made a lot of money. The opposite is true. You must have a wealth mindset before you achieve wealth.

The real secret to wiping out money problems forever is in nipping them where they are hiding—in your mind.

To be a successful entrepreneur, you have to find the match between your love and what the public wants to buy. There's always a way.

Marketing is sharing your love and passion with the people who want to hear about it.

You can't just sit there thinking positive thoughts without doing anything to turn around your finances. You must take immediate inspired action, come up with a new plan, and work it.

If you adopt an entrepreneurial mindset, it will allow you to see new opportunities pop up all of the time.

Problems create opportunities, which people often overlook. Turn the problems that you see around you into money-making opportunities.

Anyone can learn to think and act like an entrepreneur. Turn the things that you are deeply passionate about into opportunities to produce income.

The Universe can provide all kinds of new doors and windows for you to receive money through.

Elevate your thinking to understand that money can come to you in a vast, surprising, unexpected, unpredicted amount of ways.

There are ideas everywhere. A rule of thumb is, whenever you hear someone make a complaint, there's actually an idea of a potential product there!

Just like happiness, you can't pursue money. The only way to have more wealth in your life is to "attract" money to you by allowing it to flow to you.

When you realize money is a neutral force for good, and you deserve it, then you begin the process of attracting money.

Beliefs such as "money is the root of all evil" block prosperity. The lack of money is actually the root of all evil.

Money will come to you when you are ready to receive it. If you believe money can come to you instantly, effortlessly, surprisingly, unexpectedly, the Law of Attraction will match that belief and you will have money coming into your life.

You are a successful entrepreneur not when you focus on money, but when you focus on your dreams and passions, and are in love with what you do.

To be a millionaire, you must think constantly about multiple streams of income.

An economic downturn is a good time for entrepreneurs to start a business. Start-up costs are much lower in a recession than in boom periods.

It's a common misconception that it takes a lot of money to get anywhere. Not true. Even a small amount of money applied in just the right way can produce powerful results. A drop of water looks and feels harmless—but drops of water over time carved the Grand Canyon. Similarly, don't underestimate the power of a little bit of money applied in the right way.

It's vital that you do what you love. Look at your hobbies as potential ways to produce income.

Saving is not as powerful in attracting money as giving. The more money you give, from a heart of love and to wherever you feel inspired, the more you will receive.

Planning for your retirement isn't as powerful as living now with an awareness of your future. Putting off your enjoyment of life is pushing away your current prosperity.

Stocks are not as secure as acting on ideas. Money-making ideas are gifts from the Universe; act fast on them and you can prosper fast.

Practical spending isn't as wise as enthusiastic spending. When you buy something that helps you feel good, you increase your energy vibration, feel better about yourself, and tend to do more things to make more money.

You must achieve a mindset of wealth before you will ever achieve wealth itself because if you don't, you'll find yourself frequently getting close, but never quite achieving your dream.

You can't really achieve great monetary success until you follow your passion. Follow your passion, follow your enthusiasm, and success will knock on your door.

Once you realize that the spiritual and material are two sides of the same coin, you are free to have happiness as well as cash.

The Universe can provide all kinds of new doors and windows for you to receive money through. Elevate your thinking to understand that money can come to you in a vast, surprising, unexpected, unpredicted amount of ways.

The Universe is prosperous and can give you money in a wide variety of ways.

Your wealth is hiding under the very thing you are afraid to do. It's time to face your fears and take action. *Expect Miracles.*

If you turn it over to the Universe, you will be surprised and dazzled by what is delivered to you. This is where magic and miracles happen.

—DR. JOE VITALE

Magic, Miracles, and Manifestation

Miracles happen all the time—no exceptions. The fact that you are here is a miracle.

True magic occurs when you are in alignment with your life's purpose and doing what makes your heart sing.

Thoughts are sending out that magnetic signal that is drawing the parallel back to you.

We are all, on one level or another, a magnet. Everything around us is attracted to us because of us.

What you love or what you hate will be drawn to you.

We attract "junk" when we think from selfishness and fear; we attract "gold" when we think and act with love.

The thing is, you and I are different from tables, chairs, houses, and cars because we are spiritual. That's the miracle of our lives!

How we feel about money is really important, especially if we are trying to manifest more money.

You don't need to focus on money. Don't spend your time imagining how it would come to you. Allow the Universe to surprise you. There is nothing more delightful than unexpected money.

Each one of us has an inner compass. When you follow it fearlessly, you go in the direction of manifesting and attracting great wealth in your life.

What you hold in your mind with energy and focus will tend to be created in your reality. It takes a little longer to experience results because we keep changing our minds.

Don't expect the Universe to shove an elephant through your door when you have only left an opening wide enough for a gnat!

Expect success; *expect* money to come into your life and you will find it!

The magic and miracles never cease to occur, whether you see them happening or not.

If you turn it over to the Universe, you will be surprised and dazzled by what is delivered to you. This is where magic and miracles happen.

The new secret to manifesting your goals is to: Have fun. Keep smiling. Be playful. Stay grateful.

Manifesting what you want is a co-creation process. You have to take inspired action and do your bit, and trust that the Universe will kick in and will do its part. Manifestation is a joint effort.

Wherever you are right now, pause, take a deep breath, and be grateful for this moment, now.

—DR. JOE VITALE

Present Moment and Future Now

Whatever you are experiencing right now, good or bad, painful or pleasurable, will pass. This realization will help you to appreciate this moment.

Where you are now is temporary. Where you are going is eternal.

The great goal of life is to awaken and tune into this moment. And this moment is all there is.

Whatever your next goal or intention happens to be, imagine it's done and you're way past it in time.

The past is gone and the future isn't here yet. All you've got is "now." You need to awaken to the power of "now."

Where you are right now is your current reality. It is temporary. The temporary will change; your current reality will change.

You must live in the moment. Be happy right now. The incessant chasing of worldly "things" is an illusion that can keep you preoccupied and distracted from present moment happiness.

This moment is abundance. This moment is the miracle. In this moment, where abundance lives and breathes, seeing the next action and inspiration is a breeze. It's right there. Better said, it's right here.

To accelerate the process of manifesting a particular thing, you must see what you want in mind, and also feel what it would be like to already have that thing achieved.

The point of power in your life is now. This moment is your time of blazing noon.

"Nevillize" your goal. Imagine what it would feel like to already have it as achieved. Live the end result in your mind. It speeds up the Law of Attraction.

Feel the joy of having what you want—feel it right now—and you will begin to attract it to you and you to it.

You must imagine that you are already experiencing what you desire. Write it down now, with as much vivid detail and emotion, as if it's already happened.

You will have greater success in achieving your goals if you make the emotional connections in your mind, where you can feel, hear, and experience what it will be like to actually have what you're striving for.

Whatever image is in your mind, if you add feeling and emotion to it, it will manifest.

Wherever you are right now, pause, take a deep breath, and be grateful for this moment, now.

You never know what moment is the last one. Live now; when opportunities come your way, grab them. Do more smiling, hugging, sharing, crying, laughing, risking, and forgiving.

*If you can truly love everything in your life,
including people and situations that you might have
deemed to be negative, you are transforming
yourself into an enlightened being.*

—DR. JOE VITALE

Self-Awareness

You are totally, 100% responsible for all your experiences in life.

Awaken to your own internal power, to your own connection to the Divine, and act on what you are inspired to do.

Celebrate what you have already done in your life. Pause and acknowledge your achievements. This raises your sense of deservingness and increases your self-esteem.

We are all gems. We are magnificent beings. And so is everybody around you.

Devotional reading every day is a key to success. It's a way to feed your body, mind, and soul to spiritually enrich yourself.

You have the power to make a difference. The world doesn't have to change before you do. When you change, the world changes.

The unconscious/subconscious part of our mind contains the largest database of programming. *It* is running the show, not our conscious mind. As long as I just read self-help books, all I was doing was entertaining my conscious mind. I still had my subconscious to contend with.

Everything outside of yourself is an illusion, including other people. The world is a mirror, reflecting your own beliefs.

Your credentials are *You*. They are your life's experiences. Few today care about whether you have a degree. They care if you can deliver.

Forgiveness is powerful. Remember, if you don't practice forgiveness, the only person that ends up being hurt is you.

You have far more power, more ability, more talent, and more creativity than you ever realized.

If you aren't doing as well as you like, the only person standing in the way is the one you look at in the mirror every day.

We are all one. There is nothing on the outside. The outside world is really a projection of what's inside of you. The world is a mirror, forever reflecting what you are doing within yourself.

Investing in something like real estate is not as rewarding as investing in yourself.

Your mind is incredibly powerful. It not only creates your reality, but also directs your reality.

Know yourself. We are all in a trance of one sort or another. Question your deepest beliefs to awaken from within.

Life is a process of awakening. Our job is to become conscious of the unconscious process.

You are sitting in the middle of a creation. You are the creator. Look within yourself to create your outer world.

This is your moment. The sun always comes up again. The sun is rising for you right now.

Listen to your body to find out what it's trying to tell you. Your body is speaking its mind. Go ahead and have a dialog with it. This is how you heal your body and mind.

Love yourself. Accept yourself the way you are. Give yourself unconditional approval just because you're breathing...you're alive!

Money is a highly evolved spiritual tool that you can use with awareness to make a difference on this planet. Money by itself is nothing; it is we who provide meaning to money.

When you let go of your perception and judgment of a situation or a person, you free yourself.

Start right where you are. You don't have to wait for anything to change, because nothing else is going to change until you do anyway. It's all an inside job.

The great secret of life is not that you tried; it's that you kept on trying.

You must love yourself. You must have a tremendous level of acceptance of all your good qualities and be working on the qualities you want to improve.

We all have a calling. Each one of us has a role to play on this planet. When we play the instrument that is meant for us in the orchestra of life, we will be in a constant state of bliss.

The outer circumstances are not what dictate what's going on in your life. You are the one that's in control.

Blame and excuses are easy. They let you avoid responsibility. But your life is about total responsibility.

The outer world is simply a reflection of your inner world. You don't want to begin by finding

Things on the outer to love. You want to begin by finding the inner *You* to love.

The whole world is within you. As you heal yourself, the outer world heals.

Your emotions are there for a reason. There is a lesson to be learned. Get the lesson and you no longer need the experience.

The world, on many levels, is totally fine the way it is. We grow and see more spirituality within it as we awaken within us.

You can't truly love others until you love yourself. When you love yourself, you have the capacity to understand, accept, and nourish other people.

Thoughts are simply and magically part of the unfolding of the divine play called Life. To find peace, we want to be the observer of our thoughts, not the judge of our thoughts.

In order to change your thoughts, you must be detached from your thoughts and become aware that you are separate from them.

You are the first and the final authority on your life. Tune into yourself and do what's right for you. Be alert to life's gifts that come your way. Let your guard down and let life in!

Trying to change the outer is like seeing your unclean or unshaven face in the mirror and trying to clean or shave the mirror.

We all know what we want. The real key is admitting it to ourselves.

Everything that you see around you, you created from the inside of you. If you want to change the outside, don't fiddle with the outer things; fiddle with the inside of you.

We are all living here by Grace. We made it. We are still making it. You are living like Kings and Queens as compared to people in third-world countries.

What happens to you in life isn't as important as the meaning you give it.

Too many people give their power away to the economy, their job, and whatever the media is telling them, when all the while, the real power lies within themselves.

When you realize what a great gift your life is, you can be in a constant state of rapture, awe, wonder, and profound peace that helps to dissolve everything within you that is keeping you away from the beauty of this moment.

You can increase your talent just as easily as you can attract anything positive in your life. Talent isn't necessarily something we are born with, it's something we can create!

Don't be afraid to ask for help. It is not a sign of weakness. Great people are always willing to lend a hand to those who ask for help out of a sincere desire to grow.

Instead of wondering what everyone is doing, ask yourself what you are doing. How are you helping the world? How are you contributing to the betterment of the planet? All of us are here in this adventure together.

You shape the world you live in and have the power to reshape it.

Always talk about others as if they were in the same room with you, listening.

You're on an ego trip if you feel you can determine someone's motivation. We have to focus on our own connections and actions and refrain from judgments.

If you can truly love everything in your life, including people and situations that you might have deemed to be negative, you are transforming yourself into an enlightened being.

Your beliefs create your reality. To discover your beliefs regarding career, wealth, relationships, and more, look at how you feel about people who are already successful in those areas.

Your life is a projection of what is within you. Your perceptions and beliefs create your outer world.

Sources of Quoted Material

Attract Money Now:
  http://www.AttractMoneyNow.com

The Attractor Factor:
  http://amzn.to/qbItOw

The Key:
  http://www.amazon.com/Key-Missing-Secret-
  Attracting-Anything/dp/0470180765

Life's Missing Instruction Manual:
  http://amzn.to/o0Id4r

The Secret:
  http://www.thesecret.tv/

Zero Limits:
   http://www.amazon.com/Zero-Limits-Secret-Hawaiian-System/dp/0470402563

Dr. Vitale's Blog:
   http://www.mrfire.com/dr-joe-vitales-blog/

Dr. Vitale's Podcasts and Online Interview:
   http://www.mrfire.com/interviews/

The Abundance Paradigm Audio Program:
   http://www.amazon.com/The-Abundance-Paradigm-Joe-Vitale/dp/1906030332

The Awakening Course Audio Program:
   http://www.amazon.com/The-Awakening-Course-Solving-Problems/dp/1118148274

Beyond Manifestation Audio Program:
   http://www.beyondmanifestation.com/

Clearing to Attracting Money Audio Program:
   http://www.clearingtoattractmoney.com/

The Missing Secret Audio Program:
   http://www.amazon.com/The-Missing-Secret-Attraction-Attract/dp/0743576179

The Secret to Attracting Money Audio Program:
   http://www.amazon.com/The-Secret-Attracting-Money-Vitale/dp/1442300639

About the Author

Dr. Joe Vitale—once homeless but now a motivating inspirator known to his millions of fans as "Mr. Fire!"—is the world renown author of numerous bestselling books, such as *The Attractor Factor, Zero Limits, Life's Missing Instruction Manual, The Secret Prayer, Attract Money Now* (free at www.AttractMoneyNow.com), *The Awakened Millionaire,* and *The Miracle.*

He is a star in the blockbuster movie *The Secret,* as well as a dozen other films. He has recorded many bestselling audio programs, from The Missing Secret to The Zero Point. He's also the world's first self-help singer-songwriter, with sixteen albums out and many of his songs nominated for the Posi Award (considered the GRAMMYs of positive music). His latest album called *The Great Something,* inspired by legendary performer Melissa Etheridge, is available at AllHealingMusic.com.

Dr. Joe Vitale created Miracles Coaching®, The Awakening Course, The Secret Mirror, Hypnotic Writing, Advanced Ho'oponopono Certification, and many more life transforming products. He lives outside of Austin, Texas with his wife, Nerissa, and their pets.

His main website is www.MrFire.com

Join the Awakened Millionaire Movement
http://www.awakenedmillionaireacademy.com

Follow Dr. Joe Vitale:
Twitter: https://twitter.com/mrfire
Facebook: https://www.facebook.com/drjoevitale
Blog: http://blog.mrfire.com/